H A B I T A T S

FORESTS

ANITA GANERI

RSVP®

**RAINTREE
STECK-VAUGHN**
P U B L I S H E R S
The Steck-Vaughn Company

Austin, Texas

HABITATS

Coasts
Deserts
Forests
Grasslands
Islands

Mountains
Polar Regions
Rivers and Lakes
Oceans and Seas
Wetlands

Cover: Temperate rainforest trees draped with hemlock moss

Title page: A deciduous wood in autumn in Vermont

Contents page: A Mbuti pygmy hunter from the Zairean rain forest

Published by Raintree Steck-Vaughn Publishers, an imprint of Steck-Vaughn Company

Library of Congress Cataloging-in-Publication Data
Ganeri, Anita.
Forests / Anita Ganeri.
    p.   cm.—(Habitats)
Includes bibliographical references and index.
Summary: Examines different types of forests, their climate, weather, inhabitants, exploitation, and future prospects.
ISBN 0-8172-4519-7
1. Forest ecology—Juvenile literature.
2. Forests and forestry—Juvenile literature.
3. Forest conservation—Juvenile literature.
[1. Forests and forestry. 2. Forest ecology. 3. Ecology.]
I. Title. II. Series: Habitats (Austin, Tex.)
QH541.5.F6G35 1997
574.5'2642—dc20   96-8359

Printed in Italy. Bound in the United States.
1 2 3 4 5 6 7 8 9 0 01 00 99 98 97

CONTENTS

1. FORESTS OF THE WORLD

From the steamy rain forests of the tropics, to the windswept woodlands of the far north, forests play a very important part in all our lives.

They help to control the climate by absorbing the gas, carbon dioxide, that contributes to global warming. They also help to bind the soil together with their roots and prevent the soil from being washed away, or eroded. Forests are full of natural resources such as timber, food, and plants that can be used to treat life-threatening diseases.

Forests are also important to the plants and animals that they contain. They support millions of different types, or species, of plants and animals—more than any other habitat.

Trees are not the only forest plants. Beautiful orchids decorate the branches of many rain forest trees, while the floor of a temperate woodland is transformed into a carpet of flowers in the spring.

The tropical rain forests are by far the richest habitats on earth—they cover less than 7 percent of the earth's surface, yet they contain at least half

Below Map showing the extent of the world's forests. Almost half of the earth's forest cover has been destroyed in the last 10,000 years.

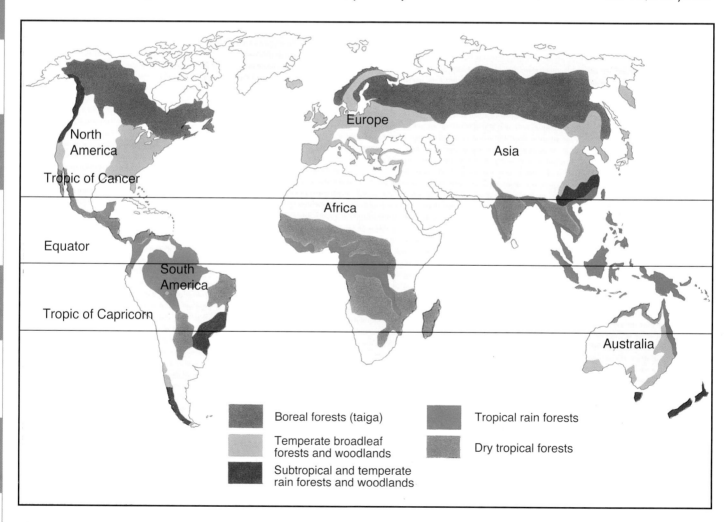

- Boreal forests (taiga)
- Temperate broadleaf forests and woodlands
- Subtropical and temperate rain forests and woodlands
- Tropical rain forests
- Dry tropical forests

A lowland tropical rain forest in Sarawak, South-east Asia. The distinctive layers of trees can be clearly seen (see page 14).

of all the world's species of plants and animals. Some scientists think they may even contain up to 90 percent of all species. The temperate and northern forests, too, are home to many rare and unusual creatures, which have adapted to life among the trees.

Some ten thousand years ago, forests covered about half of the earth's land surface. Today, they cover less than a third and are disappearing fast. Forests all over the world are being cut down and cleared for their timber and to provide farmland and building land for an ever-increasing population. In fact, the exploitation of their natural resources has led to the cutting down of forests, or deforestation on such a grand scale and at such an alarming rate that many forests are facing extinction.

Deforestation has become one of the most serious environmental problems facing the world today. If the forests disappear, so will countless species of plants and animals, many of which have not even been named or studied. Thousands of forest people will lose their traditional homes and livelihoods, and the rest of the world will lose the forest people's knowledge of the plants and animals. For these reasons it is essential to protect and preserve these extraordinary habitats.

2. TYPES OF FORESTS

Forests stretch for millions of square miles across the globe. They range from rich and abundant tropical rain forests to dry, stunted, or scrubby forests, and mangrove swamps which grow along tropical coasts. All forests have trees as their main feature, but the type and variety of the trees depends on the local climate. As a result, each forest provides its own special type of habitat and has its own unique collection of plants and animals.

The three main bands of forests around the earth are tropical rain forests, boreal (northern) forests, and temperate forests. Of the total forest cover, about 42 percent is tropical, 32 percent boreal, and 26 percent temperate. Tropical forests are dominated by broad-leaved trees, northern forests by conifers, and temperate forests by a mixture of the two. In many parts of the world, however, different types of forests exist alongside each other.

Tropical forests

Tropical forests grow between the Tropics of Cancer and Capricorn, in Asia, Africa and South America. Some smaller areas can be found in northern Australia, on several Caribbean islands, and on the island of Madagascar. There are two main types: tropical dry forests and tropical rain forests.

Left Elephants foraging among the scrubby trees of the African savannah (see opposite). Elephants can cause serious damage to the forests, uprooting young trees with their trunks.

Tropical dry forests are also known as savannah forests and are mostly found in Africa, about fifteen degrees north and south of the equator. They consist of small, shrubby trees scattered over a large area. They are an important source of firewood for the people living in and around them.

Tropical rain forests are confined to a narrow band and range from four degrees north and south of the equator. They are hot and wet all year round, providing ideal conditions in which wildlife can flourish.

There are many different kinds of tropical rain forest, including mangrove swamps along the coasts, dense lowland forests, and montane (mountain) or "cloud" forests higher on mountain slopes. The richest rain forests are the lowland forests, which are the true jungles of the world. The largest tropical rain forest grows along the banks of the Amazon River in Brazil. Known as Amazonia, it is larger than all the other rain forests put together and is twice the size of India.

Mangroves grow along swampy, tropical coasts. Their long, stiltlike roots help to anchor the mangroves firmly in the soft mud.

Temperate forests

Temperate forests grow in areas with moderate climates, between the wet, tropical forests and the cold, dry boreal forests (see page 12). They are mainly found in the northern half of the world, or northern hemisphere, stretching across central and western Europe, and in many parts of North America, central China, and Japan. But they are also found in parts of South America, southern Africa, and in southern Australia and New Zealand. However, many of the world's temperate forests have been destroyed to provide timber and farmland.

The temperate rain forests growing along the west coast of North America contain some of the biggest and oldest trees on earth. These include redwoods and giant sequoias that are more than 300 feet tall and bristlecone pines that are more than 4,800 years old.

Monkey puzzle forests
Forests of amazing, spiky monkey puzzle trees grow in southeastern Chile. The forests are home to the Pehuenche people who consider the trees sacred and rely on them for their survival. They do not cut the trees, but gather their seeds and grind them into flour. In 1976, the Chilean government declared the trees national monuments in an effort to protect them from being felled. Logging still continues, however, threatening the existence of the trees and of the Pehuenche.

All trade in monkey puzzle trees is now banned, but forests of these trees are still being destroyed by logging companies.

Giant sequoias are the most massive living things on land, reaching weights of up to 2,000 tons.

Above Huge bands of dense, coniferous forest stretch across northern North America. The most common trees in the forest are spruce, fir, and pine.

Boreal forests

The word *boreal* means northern, and these great coniferous forests stretch in an almost continuous belt across the north of Europe, Asia, and North America, reaching as far as 70° north in Siberia, Russia. In Europe and Asia, these forests are known by their Russian name of taiga, which means "dark and mysterious woodland."

To the north, boreal forests are bounded by a line that marks the farthest north that most trees will grow, the tree line—beyond it is the freezing region around the North Pole. To the south, they merge into the temperate forests and grasslands. Most boreal forests grow on land that was once covered by ice sheets.

Laurel forests of Madeira
The island of Madeira, off the Atlantic coast of Portugal, has the largest remaining patch of laurel forest in the world. In fact, the island was once almost completely covered by forest— out of an area of 173,000 acres, only 24,700 acres remain. The forest is vital to the island's water supply, providing water for drinking, for the watering of crops and, today, hydroelectric power. To protect this precious resource, the forest has been declared a national park.

3. WEATHER AND CLIMATE

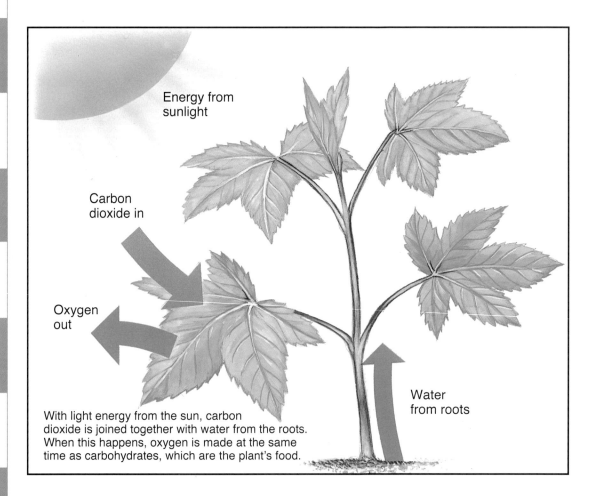

Energy from
sunlight

Carbon
dioxide in

Oxygen
out

Water
from roots

With light energy from the sun, carbon
dioxide is joined together with water from the roots.
When this happens, oxygen is made at the same
time as carbohydrates, which are the plant's food.

A diagram
showing the
process of
photosynthesis

The type of trees that grow in a particular forest, and therefore the variety of birds and animals that a particular forest can support, depends on the temperature and rainfall of the area. Like most other plants, trees make their food by a process called photosynthesis. For this, they need plenty of water and sunshine. Trees are highly adaptable and can survive in conditions which, at first sight, seem too cold or dry for them.

Year-round growth

The amazing variety of plants and animals found in the tropical rain forests is largely due to the forests' hot, humid climate. Temperatures average between 68 and 72°F all year round, and annual rainfall is between 60 and 157 inches. Afternoon thunderstorms are very common. The combination of heat and wetness creates ideal conditions for plants and trees and allows a year-round growing season. In turn, the trees and plants provide continuous food supplies for a huge variety of animals. There is no frost or drought or other seasonal changes to disrupt growth, so many rain forest trees are evergreen—they keep their leaves throughout the year.

How forests affect the climate

Not only are forests affected by the climate, but they also affect the local and global climate. During photosynthesis, their leaves absorb carbon dioxide, reducing the amount of this greenhouse gas in the air. Forests also store vast quantities of rainwater in their soils, soaking it up like a gigantic sponge and releasing it slowly into rivers and streams. This is very useful during times of drought, ensuring that the rivers and streams never completely dry out.

Trees also help to protect the land from the effects of heavy rain by binding the soil with their roots. When forests are cut down, soil erosion becomes a serious problem. In the last 20 years, floods that brought devastation to parts of India and Bangladesh can be directly linked to deforestation in the Himalayan mountains.

The devastating effect of soil erosion on a Mexican hillside, caused by deforestation.

Walk through the seasons

Temperate forests grow in places with moderate climates, that is, areas with warm summers, cool winters, and fairly even rainfall throughout the year. Many of the trees, such as oak, beech, and elm, are deciduous. This means they shed their leaves annually at the end of the growing season.

The glorious autumn colors of a deciduous forest in Vermont. This spectacular sight attracts visitors from all over the world.

11

The passing of the seasons is very noticable in a temperate forest, as the deciduous trees adapt to the changing climate. The growing season is restricted to spring and summer. In autumn, the leaves of the trees change color, from green to red and yellow, as the chemical processes that make their food "turn off" in readiness for winter.

In winter, the trees shed their leaves, their branches remaining bare until the next spring when new buds appear and the forest comes to life again. This survival mechanism means that, during the long winter months when sunlight and water are scarce, the trees do not waste precious energy trying to photosynthesize.

Coping with the cold

In the boreal forests of the far north, winters are long and harsh with temperatures falling as low as minus 94°F. These are the coldest and, despite abundant snowfall, the driest of all the forests. The growing season is extremely short, and the only trees that can survive such conditions are tough conifers, such as pine, fir, spruce, cedar, redwood, and larch. A few broad-leaved deciduous trees, such as willows and birches, are also strong or hardy enough to survive.

The conifer's triangular shape allows snow to build up on its branches and then slide off, without damaging the tree.

Conifers are ideally suited to life in the cold. They have slender, wax-coated needles instead of broad leaves to help prevent water loss through evaporation. Most keep their needles throughout the year. Conifers tend to grow close together, for protection against the cold. They are also cone shaped, which allows snow to slide off their branches easily—if the snow was permitted to build up, the branches might break under its weight.

Right The spiky needles of a spruce tree. The needles grow from small 'leaf-pegs' on the twigs. The needles' tough, waxy coating makes them resistant to drought.

Fire hazard

Fire is a constant danger in hot, dry climates, and nowhere is more at risk from fire than the forest. Some trees protect themselves from fire with a thick layer of insulating cork under their bark. Others actually rely on fire to survive. Pine trees in California need the fierce heat of a forest fire to trigger off the germination (sprouting) of their seeds. If forest fires are managed too successfully in these areas, no young trees will be able to grow to replace the old, dying ones.

The aftermath of a recent forest fire that swept through trees along the Yellowstone River in Wyoming.

4. PLANTS AND ANIMALS

Forests provide many different habitats, ranging from the forest and its community of animals and plants as a whole, called the forest ecosystem, to smaller, more specialized habitats, called microhabitats. Microhabitats can be found under tree bark or among leaf litter on the forest floor.

The animals and plants in the forest are dependant on each other for survival. Trees depend on birds and animals for pollination and seed dispersal. The animals and birds rely on the trees for food and shelter. If one part of the chain is damaged, the rest suffers too. Forests are among the most varied and complex habitats on earth. They are also among the most fragile.

Layers of life in the rain forest

A single acre of rain forest may contain as many as 200 different species of tree, compared to about ten in the same area of temperate woodland. Rain forest trees include precious hardwoods, such as teak, mahogany, and

Diagram showing the layers of growth in a rain forest

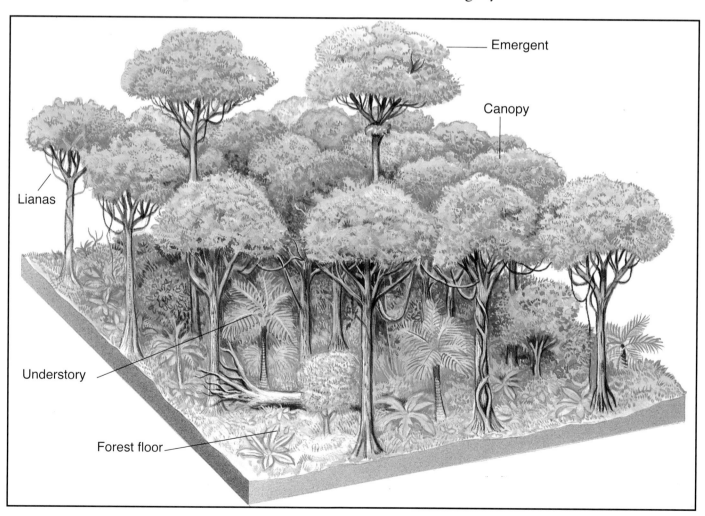

Emergent

Canopy

Lianas

Understory

Forest floor

ebony, giant kapoks, palm trees, and an impressive number of fruit trees. Many of the trees are draped in ropelike vines, called lianas. Some have spreading roots, called buttress roots, for support.

The trees grow in distinct layers, each layer having its own specific plant and animal life. A green roof of treetops, called the canopy, stretches over the forest like an umbrella, some 100 to 130 feet above ground. A few of the tallest trees poke 32 to 50 feet above the canopy. These are called emergents. Beneath the canopy is the understory, made up of smaller trees and saplings. Below this is the dim, dark world of the forest floor, covered in several inches of rotting leaves.

Creatures of the canopy

The canopy receives more rain and sun than any other part of the forest and is home to the majority of animals. These include birds, insects, monkeys, bats, snakes, lizards, frogs, and squirrels. Among the most famous inhabitants of the South American rain forest canopy are sloths and toucans. Sloths spend most of their lives hanging upside down, half asleep, from the branches. They rarely descend to the ground or have contact with other sloths, except to mate. Sloths do not spend much time cleaning themselves and allow tiny plants called algae to grow on their shaggy coats. The green color of the algae helps to camouflage them among the leaves and provides an ideal place for moths that feed on the algae to lay their eggs.

The three-toed sloth spends about 18 hours of the day hanging from a tree branch, fast asleep. The rest of its time is spent feeding.

Toucans are famous for their large, brightly colored beaks, which can reach more than 8 inches in length. A toucan's beak is extremely strong and quite light for its size, and the bird uses it to pluck fruit and insects from the branches. It also displays its beak as a warning to enemies and can be seen using it to topple other toucans off branches in a kind of wrestling game that the birds seem to enjoy.

Deadly jewels of the understory

In the understory of the South American rain forest lurk some of the most dangerous animals in the forest. These are tiny, brightly colored arrow-poison frogs, so called because local hunters tip their hunting arrows and blowpipe darts with the deadly poison from the frogs' skin. A single drop of poison is strong enough to kill a large monkey. The frogs' brilliant colors serve to advertise that they are poisonous and warn hungry predators that they are extremely dangerous to eat.

Above A toucan using its large beak to reach fruits from a nearby branch

Left The skin of the tiny arrow-poison frog contains a deadly poison that prevents the victim's breathing muscles from working.

Gardens in the sky

Few plants can be found growing beneath the rain forest canopy—there is simply not enough light to allow them to thrive. Vines have adapted to this fact and attach themselves to saplings (young trees). As the saplings grow, the vines are carried up toward the canopy and the light.

Other plants, called epiphytes, grow high up on the branches of the canopy trees. These include beautiful orchids, spiky bromeliads, mosses, and ferns. For nourishment, these "air plants" collect moisture by dangling their roots in the humid air and obtain the nutrients they need from the leaf mold (the remains of dead or decaying plants) that collects on the branches.

Pollinators and seed dispersers

The animals of the rain forest rely on the year-round growing season to provide them with a continual supply of food. In return, the trees rely on the animals for pollinating their flowers and spreading their seeds. This relationship is vital in the rain forest, where there is very little wind for scattering pollen and seeds.

The plants have many different ways of attracting the attention of insects. Some insects are attracted by flowers that are brightly colored, while others, such as butterflies, have a very good sense of smell and are drawn to sweet-smelling flowers.

The rafflesia of Southeast Asia produces the largest flower of any plant, measuring almost three feet across. It is also one of the smelliest of all flowers, reeking of rotten meat in order to attract flies that will carry off the pollen grains.

Flowers that are pollinated by birds do not need to be scented because birds have a poor sense of smell. Instead, the flowers are often brightly colored. Many are bright red—a color most insects cannot see but birds can recognize.

Animals and birds, such as howler monkeys and toucans, leave their droppings as they go in search for food. In this way the seeds of the fruit they eat are spread throughout the rain forest.

The rafflesia is a parasitic plant—it relies on a rain forest vine for nourishment. Its distinctive smell of rotting meat has led to its nickname of "stinking corpse flower."

A baby orangutan at a wildlife center in Borneo. The center introduces orphaned and captive-bred orangutans into the wild. Orangutans are threatened by the loss of their forest habitat and by capture for the illegal pet and zoo trade.

Rain forest riches
The rain forest is by far the richest habitat on earth. A 2,500-acre area of rain forest may contain about 750 different species of trees, 1,500 species of flowering plants, 400 species of birds, 150 species of butterflies, 100 species of reptiles, 60 species of amphibians, and countless insect species.

Trees in the temperate forest

The trees growing in a typical temperate woodland include beech, oak, elm, ash, horse chestnut, hazel, silver birch, and willow. A greater range of species is found in the temperate forests of Asia and North America, which contain hickories, maples, and magnolia trees, among many others.

Temperate forest trees are more widely spaced than the trees in a rain forest. This allows more sunlight to reach the forest floor, encouraging a thick undergrowth of ferns, mosses, brambles, and small shrubs. The majority of trees are deciduous, adapting to the seasons by shedding their leaves in winter.

Below A purple hairstreak butterfly feeding on an oak leaf. By laying her eggs on the oak leaves, the female ensures that the caterpillars have a ready supply of food.

Life in an oak tree

Every tree in the temperate forest is a source of food and shelter for a large community of wildlife. A single oak tree can support well over 300 different species of insects alone. Each insect is adapted for living on a particular part of the tree, such as a leaf, twig, or root.

The purple hairstreak butterfly lays its eggs on the oak leaves, which later provide food for the newly hatched caterpillars. The caterpillars of the tortrix moth roll themselves in the oak leaves to protect their bodies from predators.

Oak bark beetles lay their eggs under the oak's bark. The larvae (grubs) feed on the bark, producing long, vertical channels as they burrow between the bark and wood. Oak gall wasps lay their eggs in the buds, leaves, or roots of the oak tree. When the eggs hatch, a swelling, called a gall, grows around the grubs to protect them.

These, and the many other insect inhabitants of the oak tree, provide food for a whole host of larger creatures, including larger insects, birds, bats, and squirrels. Together they form a complex web of life— they all depend on each other in some way for their survival.

Leaf litter decomposers

In winter, the forest floor is littered with dead leaves shed by the deciduous trees. In the forest ecosystem, nothing is left to waste. The leaves are broken down by ground beetles, earthworms, fungi, and bacteria, and their valuable nutrients are recycled and returned to the soil for new plants to use.

Temperate forests have much richer soil than tropical forests, where nutrients are quickly washed from the soil by heavy rainfall. Boreal forests generally have poor soils because the dead needles that carpet the forest floor contain few nutrients and are slow to decompose, or rot.

A koala munching on eucalyptus leaves in an Australian forest. Many koalas are losing their homes because of forest fires and forest clearance to make way for farmland.

Feeding the koalas
The temperate forests of southeast Australia are home to a unique community of marsupials—mammals that carry their young in their pouches. Among these are koalas, which live almost entirely on eucalyptus trees, devouring so many of the leaves that they smell strongly of eucalyptus. The leaves contain substances that make them poisonous to the other marsupials of the forests.

Conifers in a cold climate

Boreal forests are mainly composed of conifers, which means there is far less variety of tree than in a tropical forest. A single species of conifer may cover hundreds of square miles of boreal forest.

Because conifers grow close together, little sunlight reaches the forest floor. As a result, the undergrowth is much more thinly scattered than in a temperate forest. The trees have shallow, spreading roots that allow them to take advantage of the nutrients available in the spring, when the topmost layer of soil thaws out.

Specialist feeders

Animals of the boreal forest include browsers, such as red deer and moose, so called because they browse or graze on moss and lichens. Predators, such as wolves and lynx, can also be found here, along with seed and insect eaters, including squirrels and birds. One type of bird, the crossbill, has an extraordinary crossed-over beak for prying open the scales of cones while it picks out the seeds with its tongue.

Surviving the winter

Surviving the winter is a serious problem for the animals of the northern forests. Many insect-eating birds, such as flycatchers and warblers, are summer visitors only, flying south again in the winter.

Squirrels store seeds and nuts for the long winter months. They live snug and warm in their nests. Other animals, such as bears, hibernate to avoid the cold and lack of food. During hibernation their heart and breathing rates slow down. They spend the winter in a deep sleep, living off reserves of body fat built up in the autumn when food is plentiful.

Above Lynx are well suited to life in the northern forests. They have thick, warm coats and furry toes, which makes it easier for them to walk in deep snow. They feed on small animals and birds.

Left Crossbills feed on conifer seeds, grasses, thistles, and insects such as flies and beetles. Young birds are born with uncrossed bills.

5. PEOPLE OF THE FOREST

For thousands of years, the world's forests have been home to millions of local, or indigenous, people. They live in a way which does no lasting harm to the forest, relying on it for food, fuel, medicines, and the materials that they use to build their homes and make their clothes.

Forest people have collected a vast knowledge of their surroundings, including, in the case of rain forest peoples, an invaluable understanding of medicinal plants. Unfortunately, as the forests are cleared for their timber and land, the local people as well face the destruction of their forest homes.

A further threat to their way of life comes from diseases, such as influenza and measles, brought into the forest by settlers from outside. The forest people have no natural resistance, or immunity, to these diseases, and many die from them.

Above A man carving a canoe out of a tree trunk in the Sumatran rain forest. In dense forest, it is easier to travel along a river than to push through the tangle of undergrowth.

The Penan—hunter-gatherers

Of the 150 million people living in and around the tropical rain forests, about a million are hunter-gatherers. The Penan people of Sarawak, Malaysia, are nomads, moving through the forest in search of fruit, nuts, roots, and their main animal prey of monkeys.

The Penan's traditional way of life is now threatened by the destruction of the forest by logging companies. Today, only 650 nomadic Penan remain where once they were more than 10,000 strong. In the past, they could have retreated farther into the forest, but the logging roads now reach into the heart of their home, making this impossible. In their recent efforts to block the passage of the logging trucks, the Penan have risked arrest, prison sentences, and huge fines to save the forests.

Above Penan children playing. Their centuries-old way of life is now threatened by the logging companies.

Left Blowpipes are made from hollow reeds or bamboo stems fitted inside a wooden casing with a wooden mouthpiece. Using a blowpipe, an experienced hunter can hit a target 100 feet away.

A pygmy man from Zaire hunting with a traditional bow and arrow. These hunters are expert at tracking animals through the forest.

The Mbuti—okapi hunters

The Mbuti pygmies of the Zairean rain forest live by hunting and gathering. They are experts at hunting the shy, solitary okapi, a member of the giraffe family. Unknown to western scientists until 1901, the okapi had been hunted by the Mbuti for centuries. Today, the Mbuti are using their local knowledge to help scientists study the okapi in greater detail.

Despite their small stature, the Mbuti are fearless hunters, catching okapi and royal antelope with nets and bows and arrows. The Mbuti also set out on long, dangerous hunts for elephants.

Honey is a highly prized food and a very special relationship has developed between the Mbuti and a small bird, called a honeyguide. The honeyguide leads the hunter to a hive. As a reward the hunter leaves the bird a feast of beeswax, its favorite food.

People of the Amazon

About a million native Amazonian peoples, divided into some 500 groups, live in the Amazon rain forest of South America. Each group has its own language, culture, and customs, but all share the same respect for the forest around them. Five hundred years ago, when the first Europeans arrived in South America, there were ten to fifteen million native Amazonians living in the rain forest. With their numbers greatly reduced by the destruction of their homes and the introduction of diseases to which they have no immunity, they are today struggling to preserve their lands and traditions.

The Yanomami

At about 20,000 strong, the Yanomami are the largest group of native Amazonians. They live in clearings in the rain forest on the border between Brazil and Venezuela in huge, circular houses, called *yanos*, built from tree trunks and thatched with palm leaves. About twenty families share a *yano*. Each family has its own living area and fireplace, around which the family members hang their hammocks. The open space in the center of the circle is left clear for ceremonial dancing.

A group of Yanomami. Baskets are sold or used for storing food and belongings.

The Yanomami are skilled hunters, using arrows and blow-pipe darts dipped in poison from the arrow-poison frog to kill their prey of monkeys, toucans, tapirs, and armadillos. Today, rifles have been added to the traditional hunting weapons.

About three-quarters of their food is grown in small plots close by the *yanos*. Here they raise crops, such as bananas, sweet potatoes, maize (corn), and manioc, a major part of their diet. Because the soil is poor, the plot is abandoned after two to three years and another area of land is cleared for cultivation. The abandoned plot is quickly reclaimed by the forest, and no lasting harm is done.

Yanomami men can earn great respect and glory if they prove to be good hunters. Often, they set off in small groups, but they also hunt alone, and they must follow a set of rules and customs many centuries old. For example, they never kill more prey than they need for fear of rousing the anger of the spirits, which they believe live inside every forest animal. A hunter never eats an animal he has killed himself. Instead, it is shared out among the other families in the yanos, and he receives meat from another hunter in return.

Celebrating special occasions

The native Amazonians have a strong tradition of dance and ceremony. Dances are held to celebrate special occasions, such as weddings, funerals, and harvest time. Only men are allowed to wear full ceremonial costume, including elaborate head-dresses made of macaw, toucan, or parrot feathers and necklaces and belts made of jaguar or ocelot teeth (types of jungle cat). They paint their faces and bodies with red and black plant dyes. The Wai Wai people believe that this protects them from evil spirits, which cannot see anything that is painted red.

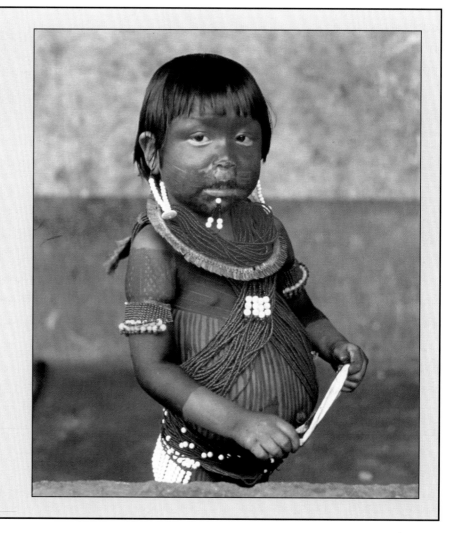

A Kayapo child. From an early age, body painting and jewelry are an important part of a native Amazonian's life. The most elaborate costumes are reserved for special ceremonial dances.

People of the northern forests

Life in the northern forests is extremely hard, yet these inhospitable regions have been home to several groups of indigenous peoples, including the Saami (Lapps) of Scandinavia and Russia, and the Chukchi, Samoyeds, and Nenets of Siberia.

These peoples are hunters, trappers, and herders, relying on reindeer, or caribou, for their raw materials and livelihoods. Like the indigenous people of tropical rain forests, they face a serious threat to their traditional lifestyle from the activities of outsiders—often representatives of companies intent on exploiting the oil and other mineral wealth of the northern region.

Reindeer herders of Lapland

Some 30,000 Saami live in Lapland, their homeland in the northern parts of Norway, Sweden, and Finland. This is wild, spectacular country, with snow-capped mountains, deep valleys, fast-flowing rivers, and dense coniferous forests. For four or five months each winter, the land is covered in a thick blanket of snow.

The Saami have lived in this region for at least 2,000 years, managing to maintain their traditional way of life.

A reindeer herder and his reindeer in the frozen wastes of northern Russia. Some reindeer are used for meat and raw materials. Other animals are raised for sale.

The forest-living Saami live a seminomadic existence, herding the forest reindeer and fishing in the many rivers and lakes. They rely on reindeer for meat, milk (from which they make cheese), and skins (from which they make clothes and tents), following the herd as it grazes on lichens and grasses. They also use tame, or domesticated, reindeer to haul sledges and to carry heavy loads and trade items made from reindeer for other goods.

In 1986, the Saami's reindeer herds were contaminated by radioactivity from the Chernobyl nuclear reactor disaster in Russia. As a result, many of the reindeer had to be destroyed, which threatened the Saami's way of life.

Migrating reindeer

Reindeer follow traditional paths in their search for pasture. In June, they migrate north to the tundra, the vast treeless plain of the Arctic, to spend the brief summer grazing. At the end of August, they gather for the return journey south, back to the forests where they will survive the long winter by living off the fat reserves they have built up during the summer. The reindeer may cover 600 miles on their journey, traveling as much as 38 miles in a day.

6. RAIN FOREST EXPLORERS

The indigenous people of the rain forest were its first explorers: the first evidence of human beings in the rain forest comes from the islands of Java and Borneo and dates back some 40,000 years. These early people lived as hunters and gatherers, as many rain forest people still do today, wandering from place to place in search of food.

By the time the first European explorers visited Amazonia about 600 years ago, the rain forest people had lived there for many hundreds, and even thousands, of years and had come to know and respect the secrets of the forest. For them it was home. For the new visitors, the rain forest was mysterious, uncharted territory, full of horrors such as cannibals, poisonous snakes, and deadly diseases.

The first European explorers
The 15th and 16th centuries were the great age of European explorers, when sailors set out on long ocean voyages to find new trade routes and territories. By the early 16th century, the Spanish had taken over much of South America, spurred on by the continent's great reserves of gold.

In 1540–42, a Spanish captain, Francisco de Orellana, was exploring the

The Spanish explorers of Central and South America sent back many reports of the strange beasts seen on their travels. As this drawing of 1597 shows, their descriptions were sometimes rather far-fetched.

rain forest when he and his men ran out of food—they had already eaten not only their rations, but their horses and hunting dogs, too. On his search to find food, Orellana discovered the world's largest river, the Amazon River, and became the first European to travel down the river to the sea.

Rubber trees

In 1735, the French scientist Charles Marie de La Condamine led an expedition to South America to measure the shape of the earth. Once there, he became fascinated by the plant and animal life of the region and stayed on for another ten years to study it. During this time he discovered that a certain rain forest tree produced a milky juice when it was cut. This juice is called latex. Rubber is made from the latex, and by the end of the 19th century rubber manufacturing had become an important industry.

However, until the middle of the 19th century, rubber trees grew only in Brazil—the country was the world's only producer of latex. But then a British botanist, Sir Henry Wickham, took some seeds out of the country, and by the early 20th century, huge estates of rubber trees, or rubber plantations, had been established in Malaysia. Since then, Malaysia has produced most of the world's natural rubber.

A woman collects latex from rubber trees in East Java. Cuts are made in the tree bark and the oozing sap collects in small bowls.

Two hundred years ago, the German naturalist Baron Alexander von Humboldt made important scientific explorations in South America.

Humboldt's travels

The English naturalist Charles Darwin called Baron Alexander von Humboldt, "the greatest scientific traveler who has ever lived." Humboldt was a German naturalist, and he combined a spirit of adventure with an interest in every aspect of natural history.

In 1799, Humboldt and the French botanist Aimé Bonpland set out on an epic voyage to South America. They traveled through dense, steamy rain forest, across alligator-infested waters, and up snow-capped volcanoes, recording everything they saw.

By the time they returned to France in 1804, the two had traveled some 40,000 miles and collected 30 chests of specimens, including 60,000 plants. Humboldt spent the next 23 years writing the first detailed account of the plants and animals of South America, a work that filled 29 volumes.

Naturalist explorers

Inspired by Humboldt's account and gripped by the new age of scientific discovery, two English naturalists, Alfred Russell Wallace and Henry Walter Bates, set off together for South America in 1848. The two were soon joined by another English naturalist, Richard Spruce.

During his eleven years in Amazonia, Bates collected more than 14,000 different species of insects, over half of which had never been seen before by European scientists. In the space of just three weeks, Wallace and Bates collected 150 species of forest butterflies alone. Spruce sent back more than 30,000 plant specimens to museums and universities all over Europe. He also studied the languages of 21 Amazonian tribes and mapped about 10,000 miles of river, traveling all the way by canoe.

The three men came close to death many times on their journeys. They fell ill with the serious diseases malaria and dysentery and were attacked on several occasions by dangerous animals. One incident involved an anaconda—a large nonvenomous snake. Late one night, Bates's canoe was attacked by the snake. It used its head to hammer a hole in the chicken coop that was being carried on the canoe and swallowed a couple of chickens.

Henry Walter Bates, one of the foremost naturalist explorers of the 19th century. Thanks to his work, thousands of species of rain forest plants and animals were brought to the attention of the world's scientists.

> ### Meeting the great apes
> *In the 1850s, the American explorer Paul du Chaillu became the first Western explorer to encounter a gorilla. The gorilla's undeserved reputation for fierceness owes much to du Chaillu's description of the ape as "fierce" and "untameable." In fact, gorillas are normally quiet and peaceful creatures living in the thick, moist rain forests of central Africa. Hunting and destruction of their rain forest habitat has made these impressive creatures an endangered species.*

Discovering the secrets of the canopy

Rain forests have been explored and studied for hundreds of years, yet we still know very little about them. In fact, scientists estimate that the majority of canopy plants and animals still have to be identified and named.

Today's explorers include zoologists (people who study animals), botanists (people who study plants), and geologists (people who study rocks and soil). They are working together in an effort to preserve and protect the community of animals and plants found in the rain forest.

One of the obstacles facing scientists is the difficulty of observing wildlife in the dense vegetation of the canopy. They now use rope-climbing techniques, more familiar among mountaineers, and construct scaffolding towers and portable walkways to uncover the secrets of the canopy.

Rain forest raft

In 1989, a group of French scientists devised a way of exploring the rain forest canopy in French Guiana. They worked from a huge inflatable, six-sided raft perched on the treetops, which was lowered gently into place by a hot-air balloon.

For a year, the scientists worked and even slept on the raft, examining plants and animals through the webbing stretched among the raft's inflatable ribs and from holes in the raft. To make them feel more at home, they named each rib after different streets in Paris.

The dense vegetation of the rain forest canopy makes exploration very difficult. Scientists are constantly finding new ways of overcoming this problem.

Electronic eyes on the rain forest

The latest technology is being used to map and monitor the ever-decreasing rain forests. An ambitious project, called the Tropical Rainforest Ecology Experiment (TREE) was recently launched in Belize, in Central America, to gauge the rate and severity of the deforestation. Three remote-sensing (signaling) devices were flown over the forest on U.S. space research aircraft to examine the landscape.

Similar sensors are due to go into space in 1998, in a series of earth-monitoring satellites. The devices transmit images of the landscape from space, showing different areas of vegetation and cleared land in different colors. Scientists in the forest itself match ground features with the radar images.

A satellite image showing wide deforestation in a part of the Amazon rain forest in Brazil. The remaining rain forest is shown in dark green and the cleared forest in light green and brown.

Ecotourists

The latest group of people to discover the wonders of the rain forests are so-called "ecotourists." These are visitors who travel as part of an organized tour, carefully supervised by a local guide. Visitors to the Perinet Reserve in Madagascar, for example, stay in huts and follow local guides along fixed trails into the forest, where they spot lemurs and other creatures found nowhere else in the world. The ecotourists bring badly needed funds to the region without damaging the environment.

An ecotourist exploring the wonders of the rain forest in Zaire. It is hoped that a greater understanding of the rain forest will lead to a greater willingness to help preserve it.

7. EXPLOITING THE FORESTS

The forests and, in particular, the rain forests, are enormously rich in natural resources. These include timber, bamboo, rattan (a climbing palm used for wickerwork), foodstuffs, rubber, oils, and resins—the list goes on and on.

We make use of many of these resources every day. Unfortunately, it is the forests' very richness and usefulness which are contributing to their destruction. Unless the resources are properly managed, they, like the forests themselves, will be gone forever.

The demand for timber

For centuries, forests have been felled for their wood. For example, in the 18th century, huge areas of European oaks were chopped down to make ships for the navy—a large warship used about 2,000 trees.

Today, the international timber trade is worth more than $40 billion a year and is responsible for about 40 percent of rain forest destruction. The worst affected areas are Southeast Asia and West Africa, but the timber companies are now looking to the Amazon and central Africa as supplies in other places run low.

Below The effects of logging in Sarawak. Commercial logging is one of the greatest single causes of tropical rain forest destruction.

A lumberjack at work in the coniferous forests of North America. Only about 10 percent of the continent's original forest cover remains.

The most valuable tropical trees are hardwoods. A single rain forest tree can be worth $1,000, and commercial logging provides valuable income for the struggling economies of many developing countries. Japan is the largest importer of tropical hardwoods, accounting for about 50 percent of the market.

In Southeast Asia, logging has led to the virtual extinction of several species of trees and the animals that depend on them for food and shelter. Huge amounts of wood are wasted in the logging process. When just a few trees are cut down, they damage about half of those left standing around them when they fall. The heavy machinery used by the loggers badly damages the land, and, by building the roads, accommodation, and services that the loggers need, the timber companies open up further hidden areas of forest, leading to greater clearance.

It is not just the rain forests that are affected—the conifer forests of western North America are disappearing fast. About 90 percent of the American part of the forest has already been felled. Most of the wood is used for plywood, paper pulp, packaging, and for making disposable diapers.

The fuelwood crisis

About half of the world's population relies on wood as fuel for heating, lighting, and cooking. They now face a crisis. Deforestation has led to a shortage of fuelwood, and the remaining fuelwood supplies are being used up rapidly. For example, women in the foothills of the Himalayas in Nepal often take a whole day to collect only enough wood to cook the evening meal. Thirty years ago, this task took an hour or so. To ease the crisis, scientists are experimenting with fast-growing trees and shrubs and with more efficient types of wood-burning stoves.

Women collecting firewood in Nepal. Forest destruction means that these women have to look further and further afield for their wood supply.

Food from the forests

Many of the foodstuffs we buy from the supermarket come from the forests. They include nuts, such as Brazil nuts from the Amazon rain forest and hazelnuts and walnuts from the temperate forests; herbs and spices such as ginger, cinnamon, nutmeg, and vanilla; and an extraordinary number of fruit and vegetables, including bananas, oranges, lemons, and pineapples.

Maize (corn), coffee, tea, cacao (from which cocoa and chocolate are produced), and rice originally grew wild in the rain forests and were later cultivated by human beings. The forest continues to produce surprises. An exciting recent discovery was a naturally caffeine-free coffee plant found in a tiny area of forest in the Comores Islands in the Indian Ocean.

Picking coffee berries in Panama. Later, the beans are separated from the skin and flesh of the berries and are sorted and roasted. They are then sold whole or ground.

The forest medicine chest

It is thought that at least 5 percent of rain forest plants, and probably many more, have medicinal qualities. The rain forest people have known about and used these plants for thousands of years. Today, their knowledge is proving invaluable to Western doctors and scientists.

About a quarter of medicines bought in pharmacies contain ingredients that were originally found in rain forest plants. Quinine is used to combat malaria, one of the biggest killers in the developing world, and comes from the bark of the South American cinchona tree. More than 1,400 plants, such as the rosy periwinkle from Madagascar, have been found with the potential to fight cancer.

The temperate forests, too, provide their share of medicines. The cancer-fighting qualities of a chemical from the bark of the Pacific yew are currently being investigated. Unfortunately, the yew is now extremely rare.

In Africa, bark and berries from rain forest trees are used to prepare cures for a wide range of illnesses.

Cattle ranching for the American fast-food industry is thought to have been responsible for the destruction of a quarter of Central America's rain forests.

Cash crops and cattle ranching

Vast areas of rain forest are being cleared to make space for growing crops that are sold abroad rather than for producing food for the local people. Known as cash crops, they include coffee, tea, sugar, oil palm, rubber and cassava.

The rain forests of Central America are being destroyed mainly to provide land for cattle ranching. Like cash crops, the ranches produce beef not for the benefit of local people but for sale abroad, mainly to feed the enormous demand for fast-food hamburgers. The ranches are extremely wasteful and uneconomic, creating poor pasture that can support only a few animals. The land is productive only for about ten years, after which time the ranchers move on to a freshly cleared area of forest.

Farming to survive

In many of the countries of Central and South America and Southeast Asia, most of the best farmland is owned by a small number of wealthy people. Millions of poor people have no land of their own and are forced to clear patches of forest in order to grow their crops and feed their families. For them, the forest is often their only means of survival.

In some countries, governments have encouraged poor people to move from overcrowded areas and to settle in the forests. The farmers clear and burn the forest and plant their crops. After two or three years, however, the poor forest soil is exhausted and the farmers have to move on. This is called slash-and-burn farming. It is destroying thousands of square miles of forest a year and is one of the major causes of rain forest deforestation. If the good farmland was shared out evenly, deforestation would be greatly reduced.

Settlers clearing land for farming in the rain forest of Guatemala. The land loses its fertility after just a few years. When this happens, the settlers must move on to another plot.

Despite studies on pandas kept in zoos, little is known about these shy animals. A greater knowledge of their behavior will help in the efforts to save them from extinction.

Endangered species

Among the most important natural resources of any forest are the numerous animals that live in it. They are also among the first to suffer when their homes are destroyed by outside influences. It is estimated that some 10 percent of rain forest species could become extinct by the year 2000 if deforestation continues at the current rate. Endangered species in the coniferous forests include the spotted owl of the northwest United States. Its nesting grounds are lost when trees are felled.

Giant pandas live in the bamboo forests of southwest China. Once widespread, there are fewer than 1,000 of them left in the wild. They feed on a type of bamboo that flowers once every hundred years and then dies. In the past, the pandas simply moved to another patch of forest when this happened. Today, when the bamboo dies, many pandas are unable to find new bamboo because more and more of the land has been taken over for farming.

Conservation groups all over the world have come together to help the Chinese government set up panda reserves in an effort to try to save these creatures from extinction. For the past 35 years, the panda has been the symbol of the World Wildlife Federation (WWF).

8. FORESTS IN THE FUTURE

Fifty years ago, the rain forests were twice the size they are today. The remaining half has been cleared by logging and mining companies, ranchers, and farmers. If the destruction continues at its present rate, there will be no rain forests left in another 20 years' time.

Other forests are suffering, too. Around the world about a million acres of forest are cleared or destroyed each week. The great coniferous forests of North America are disappearing quickly, and only a fraction of the original temperate forests of Europe remain. Saving the forests, their people, wildlife, and resources has become one of the major challenges facing the people of the world today.

A scar on the landscape—destruction of the Amazon rain forest for manganese ore mining in Brazil.

Cork bark being stacked. Because cork is absorbent, heat-resistant, and hard-wearing, it is used for bottle corks, table mats, and floor tiles.

Managing the forests

One of the best ways of preserving the forests is to use their resources sustainably. This means taking only as much of a product as the forest can naturally afford to give. Local people have been practicing this form of forest management for centuries. In the Mediterranean, for example, the bark of cork oaks is regularly stripped off and harvested without harming the trees. The bark takes a few years to regrow and can then be harvested again.

The traditional practice of agroforestry is another way of benefiting from the forests without harming them. Crops and livestock are raised alongside forest trees, greatly increasing the productivity of the land. The Chagga people, living on the slopes of Mount Kilimanjaro in Tanzania, even copy the natural structure of the rainforest. They grow their crops in layers, planting first the tallest, such as guava, papaya and bananas, then coffee bushes, then vegetables in front of them.

In the Amazon rain forest, people have set up "extractive reserves" in which they harvest the forest's products, such as rubber, spices, oils, and Brazil nuts, in a way that allows the forest to replenish itself naturally.

At the Earth Summit held in Rio de Janeiro in June 1992, world leaders met to work out how best to stop the destruction of the worldwide environment. Sustainability was high on the agenda, with a view to ensuring that timber imports, of tropical hardwoods in particular, came only from sustainable sources.

Right A tree farmer in the Amazon rain forest. For centuries, local people have used the forest's resources in a sustainable way.

Waldsterben—"forest death"

Vast areas of temperate forest in Europe and North America are affected by a mysterious condition called Waldsterben—*the German word for "forest death." Millions of trees are dead or dying. Scientists now believe that pollution from motor vehicles, power stations, and industry is to blame. The smoke and fumes mix with moisture in the air, and a weak acid is formed. This can be blown for hundreds of miles by the wind before falling to the ground as acid rain, poisoning the trees.*

This once healthy forest of fir trees in Europe has been killed by a lethal combination of air pollution and acid rain.

43

Saving the forests

All over the world scientists, conservationists, governments, and local people are attempting to halt the destruction of the forests and to preserve them for the future. In many countries, large areas of forests have been turned into national parks. These are intended as safe havens for local people and wildlife, although not all are adequately protected.

In many of these parks, hunting, logging, or any other human activity is forbidden. However, there may be a zone around the central area in which the local people are allowed to have access to the forest's resources. More than 500 million acres of forests of all types are now protected.

Various treaties and plans have also been put into action to protect the forests. In 1987, the Tropical Forestry Action Plan (TFAP) was set up by the World Bank and the United Nations with the aim of increasing the amount of aid money spent on the tropical rain forests. Many conservationists believe that the TFAP will have little effect because it does not address the issue of deforestation.

Tree replanting programs, such as this one in Nepal, have been set up to restore the forests.

The International Tropical Timber Agreement (ITTA), on the other hand, has been greeted by conservationists as the best way of controlling the international trade in tropical timber. It came into effect in 1985. Its aims are put into action by the International Tropical Timber Organization (ITTO) in Tokyo, Japan, which brings together representatives from timber companies and from countries with tropical forests to discuss the problems.

ITTO has had some success. For example, in 1989, Thailand banned logging after a series of disastrous landslides caused by deforestation. Other countries have since followed Thailand's lead, although illegal logging remains a serious problem.

People power

Local people are fighting to conserve their forests. In the 1980s, Chico Mendes, the head of the rubber tappers' union in Acre, Brazil, led a campaign against the destruction of the rain forest by cattle ranchers. His campaign became unpopular with the ranchers, and he was later murdered. However, the rubber tappers' union continues to fight for its rights today.

In India, where wood is a major source of fuel, village women are active in the Chipko movement, hugging the trees in their local forest to stop them being cut down. They have also begun to replant trees, reaching a total of three million trees in just five years.

Whether local woodland or Amazonian rain forest, the need to protect the world's forests is greater than ever. And every one of us can play a part, by making sure that we buy only sustainable forest products. With good management and greater public awareness, it should be possible to save the forests and to preserve them for the benefit of the wildlife, local people, and the rest of the world.

Penan tribespeople blocking a road used by loggers in Sarawak. They are prepared to risk arrest, fines, and even imprisonment to save their forest home.

Glossary

Adapted   Changed to suit or fit different conditions.

Amphibians   Animals that live on land and in water.

Botanist   Someone who studies plant life.

Broad-leaved trees   Trees other than conifers, having broad rather than needle-shaped leaves.

Camouflage   To disguise the appearance so as not to be easily seen.

Climate   The weather conditions of a place or country.

Community   The group of animals or people living in an area.

Conifers   Trees that bear cones and needle-like evergreen leaves.

Conservationists   People who work to stop the countryside from being spoiled or lost.

Deciduous   Describes trees that shed their leaves annually.

Deforestation   The clearing away of trees from forests.

Degrees   Distances measured north and south of the equator and used to define points on the earth's surface.

Ecosystem   The system involving the way in which a community of animals and plants relates to its surroundings.

Equator   An imaginary line around the earth, halfway between the North and South poles.

Evaporation   The changing of a liquid into a gas. For example, water changes to water vapor when heated.

Exploiting   Making use of something without regard or benefit to others.

Extinction   When a species dies out completely.

Global warming   The rise in temperature over the earth's surface. Scientists believe greenhouse gases are the cause of global warming.

Grasslands   Land on which grass is the main type of plant life.

Greenhouse gas   A gas in the atmosphere that traps the sun's heat and causes the warming of the earth's surface.

Habitat   The natural home of an animal or plant.

Hardwoods   The wood of broad-leaved trees, such as oak, mahogany, and teak.

Hydroelectric power   Electricity generated from the power of falling water.

Leaf litter   The layer of leaves and twigs on the ground in a forest.

Mammals   Animals whose females give birth to live young, which they feed with milk from their bodies.

Mangrove   A type of tropical tree that forms dense forests along coasts.

Naturalist   Someone who studies animal and plant life.

Nutrients   Substances essential for growth.

Orchids   Types of plants with brightly colored or unusually shaped flowers.

Parasitic   Describes an animal or plant that lives on another.

Photosynthesis   The process by which green plants use sunlight to turn water and the gas carbon dioxide into food.

Pollination   The transfer of pollen from one flower to another flower.

Predators   Birds or animals that attack and kill others for food.

Reptiles   Animals such as lizards, snakes, or turtles that have scaly skin.

Seed dispersal   The spreading of seeds to other parts of the forest.

Shrubs   Small bushes or woody plants.

Species   A group of plants or creatures with similar features.

Temperate   Areas of the earth between the tropics and the North and South poles, which are mild or moderate in temperature.

Tropics   The hot region between two imaginary circles running around the earth. These circles are known as the Tropic of Cancer and the Tropic of Capricorn.

Books to Read and Further Information

Books to Read:

Coote, Roger, ed. *Atlas of the Environment*. Milwaukee: Raintree Steck-Vaughn, 1992

Dixon, Dougal. *The Changing Earth*. Young Geographer. New York: Thomson Learning, 1993.

Fleisher, Paul. *Ecology A to Z*. New York: Dillon Press, 1994.

Gallant, Roy A. *Earth's Vanishing Forests*. New York: Macmillan Children's Books, 1992.

Javna, John. *Fifty Simple Things Kids Can Do to Save the Earth*. Kansas City, MO: Andrews & McMeel, 1990.

Lessem, Don. *Inside the Amazing Amazon*. New York: Crown Publishing Group, 1995.

Morrison, Marion. *The Amazon Rain Forest and Its People*. New York: Thomson Learning, 1993.

Tesar, Jenny. *Endangered Habitats*. Our Fragile Planet. New York: Facts on File, 1992.

Useful Addresses:

For further information about habitats that may be under threat, contact the following environmental organizations:

Fish and Wildlife Service, Department of the Interior, Washington, DC 20420

Friends of the Earth (U.S.A.), 218 D Street SE, Washington, DC 20003

Greenpeace U.S.A., 1436 U Street NW, Washington, DC 20009

National Audubon Society, National Education Office, R.R. #1, Box 171, Sharon, CT 06069

National Oceanic and Atmospheric Administration, Department of Commerce, Washington, DC 20230

World Wildlife Fund, 1250 24th Street NW, Washington, DC 20037

Picture acknowledgments

Bruce Coleman/Francisco J Erize 8(left), /Luiz Claudio Marigo 16(top), /MPL Fogden 16(bottom), /Erwin and Peggy Bauer 17, /Hans Reinhard 19(top), /Jane Burton 19(bottom), /Joseph Van Wormer 20, /Luiz Claudio Marigo 25, /Alain Compost 29, /Staffan Widstrand 33(bottom), /Luiz Claudio Marigo 41; Environmental Picture Library/Nigel Dickinson 5, /C Jones 23(above), /H Girardet 26, /Mark Warford 27, /N Dickinson 34, /Irene R Lengui 37, /Herbert Girardet 38, /S Whiteborne 42, /Herbert Girardet 43(top), /Alex Olah 44, /Jeff Libman 45; Mary Evans 28, 30, 31; Eye Ubiquitous/Jonathan Prangnell contents page, /Mike Southern 6, /L Fordyce 9, /DC Maybury 18, /Bennett Dean 22, /Jonathan Prangnell 24, /Tim Page 36(bottom), /Julia Waterlow 40; NHPA/David Woodfall 7; Science Photo Library/David Parker 32, /Geospace 33(top); Still Pictures/David Drain (cover); Tony Stone/Glen Allison title page, /Liz Hymans 8(right), /Robert Frerck 11(top), /Glen Allison 11(bottom), /Arnulf Husmo 12, /Randy Wells 13(top), /David Maisel 13, /Norbert Wu 15, /Reinhard Siegel 21(top), /Wayne Lankinen 21(bottom), /Paul Chesley 23(bottom), 35, /David Sutherland 36(top), /David Hiser 39, /Oliver Strewe 43(bottom). Maps and diagrams on pages 4 and 14 are by Peter Bull.

INDEX

Numbers in **bold** refer to photographs

48